ANTS IN MY PANTS
Woodstock Poems

RICARDO L GARCÍA

Credits: Cover image by **Sharon J García**
Front cover layout by **Britney Tonniges**
Reading/editing by **Raymond J Rodrigues**

Copyright © 2016 Ricardo L Garcia

All rights reserved.

ISBN: 0615649114

ISBN 13: 9780615649115

*For my brother Robert, a good man
with the heart of a poet*

Contents

I

Ants in My Pants	1
On Woodstock Avenue	2
Groovy Died Today	3
Penny for Your Thoughts	4
Freudian Slips	5
Go There	6
Baggy Ass Pants	8
Digging Fence Post Holes	9
A Desperate Race	11

II

Outside Man	15
Goodnight, Mr. Brunet	17
Gravity	20
Able-bodied Feat	21
Water Flowed Up	22
On the Dandelion	23
Outside Prints	25
Turkey Jerky	26
No Regrets	27
Skittish Roadrunner	28
Call to Order	29
The Spunky Wren	30

III

Fun to See	35
Walking by Lilacs	36
Unlikely Places	38
Light and Easy	39
Tap the Sky	40
Careless Wish	41
Shaking Painting	42
Authentic Antiques	43
So Little Time	45
Old Cottonwoods	46

IV

Mother's Pall Malls	49
The Price of Big Boy Toys	51
Booting a Bike Tire	57
New Year's Eve Bonfire	59
All Was Well	62
Matters of Fact	65
Grandfather Joe	68
Breaking the Seal	69
From the Lamp Post	73
A Jump-Start	75
Hanging On	77

PART I

Ants in My Pants
I had ants in my pants
and wasn't fit to sit
'cuz they bit and bit
my tender butt at will
for sitting on their hill.
I scooted to my brother,
who dashed me to Mother,
who pulled off my pants
and brushed off the ants
to make them
scurry in a hurry
across the wooden floor
and out the kitchen door.
She swatted me a hard one,
tough love for her baby son:
"Watch where you sit,
and you won't get bit."

On Woodstock Avenue
We stood in our yards watching the grass grow
over our respective lawns, and agreed,
her lawn is greener than mine, it was so,
although neither did much but add new seed.
The grass is greener on her side of the fence
here where I live on Woodstock Avenue,
and I'm sure it's more than envy or pretense,
even from my neighbor's point-of-view.
I see polar values in the hue,
her grass superior, mine inferior,
but why should deeper color render more value?
With that standard, Africans would be superior
and Europeans would pale in comparison.
There's an intriguing thought, as if our worth
can be stuffed in some burdensome
casing given to us at our birth.
I'd like to think there's no single marker,
the good is more than degrees of color,
in our lawns, I mean, lighter or darker,
they're as different as a paper to a silver dollar.

Groovy Died Today
(1937-2012)

Disk jockey Silent Sam just said,
marvelous old man Groovy is dead,
he suffered from irrelevance
in virtual time with hardly a chance
to beat the bum rap of old hat,
along with *jive turkey* and *hep cat*,
long gone the way of *a-okay*,
keen, snazzy, and *classy*—all passé.

Groovy was buried in the lexicon
of neat notions of past phenomenon,
out of orbit, out of sync with the time
of noisy music, poems without rhyme.
He was a cool vibe in the groove,
twisting hey-nonny-nonny on the move,
du-wopping with the *zeitgeist*:
you're okay, I'm okay, and no one can heist
the mood of the moment, the feel of swell
nuking every bead, bongo, and bell.

Gone are the days of wine and roses,
when feeling groovy was more than poses
of flower children surfing the beach,
when we strove to stretch beyond our reach
to do our own thing, but don't forget the rest
of our brothers and sisters. That's the test,
be good to others—that's the grooviest.

Ah, Groovy, chic, classy and cool,
we kids of the Sixties will miss you.

Penny for Your Thoughts
Jogging along on my mid-morning run
I spied a penny, the head of Lincoln
wedged in the gutter between the concrete
and the asphalt at the brink of the street.
Thumbed off the grit from the penny's tail
where Lincoln sat in his Memorial,
telling of a nation conceived in liberty,
with malice toward none, and charity
for all as Dr. King reminded us
in 1963, telling the chorus
of kindred spirits of all races,
at the Memorial from many places,
about a recurring hope that traces
its deep roots in the American Dream,
that the lamp of equality will beam
and provide light so none of God's children
will be judged by the color of their skin.
Clutched the gritty penny in my hand
to even out change at the coffee stand,
or plunk into a donation jar
at the cash register next time I gas the car.

Freudian Slips
Once I read
some savants said
Sigmund Freud was
wrong in many ways
tho' he sounded good
in bygone days.
Once I read
Sigmund Freud said
here's the key
to be happy:
find people to love,
and work to love—
sounds good to me.

Go There

My truancy started in math class
when I heard Miss Cornay say,
"Pi R Square," and I didn't care
to sass "pies are round,"
the fun gone in popping wisecracks
and causing clashes,
I couldn't concentrate and was bound
to ditch between classes.

Stole through the gym out the school's
back door, though stealth wasn't needed,
I wouldn't be missed, my truancy unheeded.
Crossed the prairie toward the mesa
to a place I'd found last summer
where a creek trickled through a thicket
of scrub oak trees and chokecherry bushes.

Climbed astride a leaning scrub oak
cozy with magpies clambering on branches,
pecking at acorns difficult to reach,
poking and eating, or letting them fall.
Below, squirrels scurried to snatch the acorns,
stuffing their cheeks, then hoarding them
in handy holes, or cracks in the ground,
anywhere they could later be found.

Go There

The magpies, content to gobble and eat,
flitted about, pecking and raising a stir
heedless to the snow December would incur.

While I watched the magpies and squirrels,
cool in the trees though barely a breeze,
sun high in the sky, a rooster crowed
somewhere in town, broaching me softly
where I sat as close to perfect
as one can get. Whatever was winding
in my mind sprung free.

At different ages, stages, and states,
I have returned there many times,
not school but *there* without feeling the fool.

Baggy Ass Pants
At the counter of the Log Cabin Café
I heard the young waitress say:
"N-a-a-aw! That ain't true,
you're pullin' my leg, ain't you?"

The cowboy sighed before he replied:
"If it wasn't true, I wouldn't tell you
the kid's baggy-ass pants saved him
when the rat'ler bit at his butt
and clenched a mouthful of denim.

Then I took the rat'ler by the tail,
yanked hard and threw it,
watching it sail pretty-like
over the trail,
tumblin' down the slope
like a scrap of ol' rope."

Digging Fence Post Holes

Out to the alfalfa field to build a fence,
posthole diggers in back of the pickup,
water jugs, pistol, and the two of us
up front. We had already eyeballed
the fence line, marking each corner
with a pile of pebbles, a rectangular idea
where the hills folded onto the prairie.

Already, we'd measured the distance
between posts, nothing fancy, three
long strides in-between, and marked
a place with a rock for each.

Now to the hard work, digging each hole
deep enough to stand a juniper pole
so it wouldn't fall once wire was stretched
from post-to-post to define the idea,
fence-in the alfalfa, fence-out the elk.

We took turns jamming the posthole diggers
into the ground, then pulling apart the handles,
lifting the dirt wedged between their blades,
tossing the dirt, making mounds to use
for backfill to shove back into the holes
and tamp to buttress the juniper poles.

Digging Fence Post Holes

Jamming down the diggers to punch holes
was work enough in loamy soil,
here rocks resided an inch or so below
the sandy surface. We jammed-and-lifted,
blistering our palms to dig one hole.

At this rate, we'd take a week to dig
enough holes to build the fence, if we could
fend off the fatigue, the gnats nipping
at our sweaty necks, and the rattlers
we scared-off with the pistol.

Mostly, it was our great need for water
told us our work was folly,
something the perennial gnats
and prairie rattlers had tried to tell us:
the barbed fence wouldn't keep out the elk
anymore than it would the pesky critters
that claimed a right to be there.

A Desperate Race

The lizard ran in the rut to keep ahead
of the tractor tire's heavy tread
that rolled in the same rut at a steady pace,
coaxing the lizard into a desperate race.

The lizard slowed, the tire maintained
its heavy-treaded rate and yet gained
on the tired lizard, rolling over it,
crushing the lumbering lizard to win
a deadly race neither chose to be in.

The boy driving the tractor was aware
the race was grim and still didn't care,
his concerns were to stay the steady pace
steering the tire in the rut as a base
aligned with the previous pull of the plow
around the wind-swept pasture—that's how
he plowed in a circle to be sure
to reduce erosion on the land's contour.

I was that boy driving the tractor
and will admit to the thoughtless error
of assuming the lizard could think to climb
over the rut's bank, if it had the mind.

PART II

PART II

Outside Man
He stood in the middle of the street
midst passing cars and double-
parked delivery trucks at ten a.m.
beside the open manhole intent on
clearing last winter's debris from
clogging culverts and keeping the
flow. A floppy Fedora sat atop his
forehead as he worked in the outfit
of a man who cocks his hat anyway
he wants. At first, I thought he was
a young man dancing between the
clattering machines tending dials
and adjusting gauges, returning to
the open manhole to hear himself
talk to the men below. When I drew
closer and saw his gnarled hands,
fretted brow and salt-and-pepper
temples, I saw he was growing old,
like me, though much more graceful,
lively and limber not working at all—
more like playing, engaged in the
task at hand, slow but sure, one step-
at-a-time, getting the job done right
so as not to come back a second time.

Outside Man

Outside man, old-time miners would
call him, preferring to take much lower
wages rather than burrow below for higher
to muck in the sludge of last winter's waste
shut-out from sunlight, fresh air, and the
passing parade of sprite women in knee-
high skirts and low-cut blouses, cantering
by on svelte, shaved legs, ankles wobbling
in their high-heel shoes. He was absorbed
in a lucid performance honed overtime,
disciplined to save effort in graceful steps
or standing still, poised in a baggy flannel
shirt, denim trousers, work boots scuffed
yet clean, ready for underground men to
call to flip a switch or jerk the rotor chain.
I probably gave him too much, the way
he gave himself the cocky hat and light-
footed stance in the middle of the street
at ten a.m. all dressed up for the dance.
But, I stayed and watched for what
would be next, how it would all end.

Goodnight, Mr. Brunet

Last of a tired team to be dropped off,
I was ready to call it a day,
ending a debate trip where we'd done okay
winning trophies for impromptu events,
our debate coach proud of us, buying steaks
at a fine café at his own expense.

Walter Brunet was our speech instructor
who donated time and money to drive us
to tournaments, elated in his flashy car,
a two-tone pink and red De Soto hardtop,
sleek finned-fenders and a chrome-filled grill,
blinkers to signal turns, taillights to flash a stop.

"Enjoy the trip?" He asked, steering the De Soto
into the driveway. "Uh, huh," I managed to say,
shoving the door open, the car slowing to stop,
  "You must, you know?"
  "Know what?"
  "Enjoy every minute you've got."

He reached to the bottom, left side of his seat,
pulled a lever and smiled, "It's open. The trunk."
I pivoted to my feet, forgetting
to shut the door, which I often did
scampering to the open trunk. Grabbed my
suitcase, slammed the trunk lid shut, catching
Mr. Brunet in contention, which he often did.

Goodnight, Mr. Brunet

"You're wrong to assert there's not two sides
to the argument," he insisted, barely audible
over the whoosh of the closing trunk lid.
I peered into the doorframe I'd left open,
"Yep! Right side! Wrong side. Black and white.
My Dad. Others I know. Fought for unions,
the right to strike. To withhold the only asset
they have ¾ their labor. There's one right side."

His hands hung over the steering wheel,
face staring at the lights glaring off
the glass windows on the garage doors:
"Their leaders have been corrupted, calling
for national strikes to settle local disputes
during the peak of the War when labor
was needed to keep the factories going."

Dandily dressed in buttoned vest, wool suit,
open-collar shirt and scarf instead of tie,
jade cuff links and Gucci shoes,
Walter Brunet was a fragile man to me,
sensitive, guarded, easy to bruise,
never flippant yet able to talk
on topics of any kind, engaging
in the life of the inquiring mind.

"Black? White? What's right? More like gray,
a mix of the two, shades in-between,

the proposition targets leaders who use
their influence to promote selfish interests
rather than the greater good."

He had a point, only my Dad would say
the leaders got carried away, using
their political pull to line their pockets,
forgetting why unions were formed.
"Gotta go." I insisted. "You may be right,
we could argue the issues all night."

Goodnight, Mr. Brunet

He opened his door, starting to stand,
craving to talk to fill a gap deeper
than the many sides of a debate,
yet hesitated, reluctant to speak
as if lost for words or carefully
weighing his thoughts, as he would often
advise, "make sure brain's in gear
before putting tongue in motion."

Then, he sat down, easing into the seat,
shutting his door. "*Touché,*" he quipped,
forcing me to hesitate, waiting for another
injection of a counterpoint when
he had none. He didn't crave debate
to chalk up another score for his side,
he craved to fill a void with more
than I could provide. Instead,
he said, "don't slam the door. "

Gravity
What goes up
can come
down
and conk your crown,
as Sir Isaac Newton found
when he sat on the ground
beneath an apple tree
to ponder gravity—
an apple fell on his head,
good thing it wasn't lead.

Able-bodied Feat
Outside a small Texas town, three white men
spied a black man walking with a limp,
they stopped to offer him a lift and then
beat him to death, reveling in triumph.
They tied him to their truck, folks remembered,
and dragged him down the town's main street
until he was partially dismembered,
then, they u-turned up the street to repeat
their proud parade—an able-bodied feat.
The parade pulled-in a curious crowd
to watch the feat fizz out on a patch of sod
while folks stood stolidly as decorum allowed,
none apparently too glad or sad to laud
the able-bodied feat though I would applaud
a means to justify the ways of man to God.

Water Flowed Up
Driving seventy miles-per-hour
heading west on Interstate-Eighty
I passed beneath a bridge and saw the power
of a water-drop at high velocity
smacking my windshield and flowing upward,
shoved by the headwind into narrow vines
pronging away from the mother-drop toward
pinpoint beads ending in watery lines.
Each bead bubbled, then vaporized away,
leaving the windshield clean and clear as before.
The water-drop flowed upwards, I'd say,
at seventy contrary to the lore
water falls down. Here it flowed up,
dispersing on the windshield of my truck.

On the Dandelion
If you set aside the rhetoric and cant,
when is a plant a weed? A weed a plant?

Consider the much-maligned dandelion
popping up crops of green and golden tine
on meadows, range-lands, lawns, and river banks,
encircling parks, ponds, pools, and stock tanks.

It flowers anywhere it pleases,
spreading by sprouts and seeds in breezes,
thriving in sundry sorts of soils
in greenery that grows straight or coils
most anywhere on North American dirt,
except parts of the Sonoran Desert.

Consider the practical use of its roots,
when well ground, they make fine substitutes
for coffee, laxatives, and heartburn pills,
providing a warm drink or low Rx bills.

Its flowers fried in batter are tasty
and make good wine or tea, if not hasty,
you have to ferment the flowers for wine,
or to make tea, dry them out on a line.

Its long leaves make a savory salad,
add oil, onions, and salt to make it less pallid,
and, of course, if you're a cuisine Houdini
you'll add peppers, mushrooms, and zucchini.

On the Dandelion

There are other uses for the dandelion
besides warm drinks, medicines, and wine,
bees use it to make honey, cows for food,
so why, oh why is there an organized brood
of lawn mowers and exterminators,
simpering self-serving annihilators
hell-bent on eradicating the plant
without considering the dandelion's slant?

They say, it's just a wild, wicked weed,
but that's not true, if you desperately need
a lucid laxative or heartburn pills,
or warm coffee or tea to kill the chills,

and, every bootlegging, moonshiner knows
that dandelion wine works fine in the throes
of prancing, romancing, and dancing the jig,
there's no substitute for a swig
of that much-maligned dandelion wine
popping up in a crop of green, golden tine.

Outside Prints

Prints outside the patio door
on the snow covered floor
of a grackle or jay
already here gone his way
seeking seeds, discarded food,
prompts my pensive mood,
toasty warm here in my chair,
bitter, biting cold out there.

Next time I'm grinding my teeth
whining about a supposed grief,
cursing the dark of the night
pining over a petty plight,
and I'm griping much too hard,
remind me of the frozen yard
and prints outside the patio door
on the snow covered floor.

Turkey Jerky

Do try the tasty turkey jerky
down in Duke City Albuquerque
where the turkey are fed on a mattress
of tumbleweed and prickly pear cactus,
t*ortillas* and red *chili* powder
sautéed in a bowl of tartar clam chowder.

Hey, y'all! I wouldn't jest or joke
or take a poke at Albuquerque folk
just 'cause it's still against the law
to ax, shoot, hatchet, or take a hacksaw
to a rabbit on Central Avenue,
or anywhere in the City's purview.

If needed, you can kill the rabbit, indeed,
by demonstrating you've a dire need,
such as:
you're hungry and too skinny for your pants,
worse, you've eaten all the spiders and ants
living in your *portal* in Albuquerque,
and last, you're allergic to turkey jerky.

No Regrets

The bare branches of the flowering plum
burst out first with buds in the early spring,
unfolding under the warm morning sun,
yielding azure and pink petals to bring
an array of colors over the tree,
till the leaves loom largely, the blossoms fall,
and sprinkle the lawn. You'll see
tiny plums prickle the branches overall.
Come September, the cowbirds arrive
to gorge on the plums, a Labor Day binge,
till they're too fat to fly, too drunk to dive,
but you'll not spot remorse, not even a tinge
or hint of regret for their drunken spree
while clinging to and cluttering the tree.

Skittish Roadrunner
The roadrunner skitters and stops,
skitters again across the lawn
hunting lizards, bug carcasses,
or whatever he comes upon.
Each time he stops, he cocks his head
and pricks up his tail like a deer,
warning others who follow his tread
a potent predator may be near.
If he doesn't spy predators
on the grass, ground, or in the air,
nor other rousting roadrunners
foraging with similar care,
he lowers his tail to the ground
and proceeds to skitter around.

Call to Order

Returning robins huddled atop a tree
high above roofs of neighborhood homes,
somewhat puffed to fend off the nippy chill
of this mid-March day when the sun slips
in-and-out the clouds, flirting with spring.

As the robins snuggled in their huddle,
one raised its head and whistled sharply:
"Fu-u-eet!" The others noted the whistle,
raising, cocking their heads as though mulling
the message, the pros and cons, the pertinence
to their interests and the greater good.

Mulling done, they tucked heads in puffy breasts
till another raised its beak and whistled:
"Fu-u-ett!" Again the meditative head tilts
and the pensive pauses after the whistle
before tucking heads back into breasts,
round-robin each took its turn
till all had been said that needed saying.

Meeting adjourned, they leapt in unison,
forming a small, dark cloud against the sky's
gray, nippy air. Then each broke away
flying its separate way to keep counsel
for another day.

The Spunky Wren

The spunky wren hopped over my deck
onto the rail, puffed himself, preened,
and puffed himself again,
really rotund, robust, and over-scale.

More of a powder puff than large bird,
he warbled into the abyss of trees
emulating tenors he'd never heard,
singing out his heart in a swelling breeze
of smooth sounds a likely mate would hear
to be notes of a lover and draw near.

None came.
More than smooth notes were required,
so he flew to the old house, high on an ash,
clearing last year's twigs and grass till he tired.
He rested, less full of flash-and-dash,
yet, more intent on attracting a mate,
he returned to the task, adding new grass,
more twigs to the old house. Now, he could wait.

None came.
Smooth notes and a refurbished nest
did little to muster a willing mate,
though he preened, cleaned, and sang his best,
there was hardly more he could contrive for bait.

While I pondered how luck seemed so unkind,
a squirrel skittered to the base of the ash tree
and climbed rapidly, one object in mind,
to raid the house in clear view of wren and me.

The Spunky Wren

Swoosh—he swooped at the climbing squirrel!
It slipped around to the back of the tree,
wren darted to the backside in a twirl,
squirrel scrambled down, scurrying to flee
wren's swift swoops and piercing head-pecks!

Pit! Pit! Wren pricked the squirrel,
teaching it to keep away, to mind its treks
next time it thinks to give wren's house a whirl.
Squirrel jumped, hitting the ground in a rush.
Pit! Pit! Wren continued the head attack
chasing the squirrel to skulk under the brush.

With all the commotion, I forgot to note
a female hovered about the wren's place,
a stirring signal of her choice, her vote
to move-in and make the house a cozy space.

After all that, I rarely saw the wren,
except when he foraged bugs and larvae,
combing the backyard below his cozy den,
even then, he didn't stray far from his tree.

He stayed with his mate after incubation,
teaching their fledgling to sing, hunt, and fly,
engaged in a tender yet tough incantation
where the fledgling had no choice but to try.

One autumn day he ended their stay,
without so much as a chirp, they'd flown away.
I came to admire that spunky wren
and hoped he would cross my path again.

PART III

PART III

Fun to See
Thus I make a rush
to throw that discus,

for a Frisbee
is fun to see

flying in the sky
floating by-and-by

while your dog Sadie,
also fun to see,

shoots like a bullet
and jumps to catch it

as it spins around
before hitting ground.

Walking by Lilacs

A whiff of perfume caused me to stop my walk
by the lilac bushes to smell their blooming buds
flourishing in dark purples almost burgundy,
others in softer, lighter shades of pink and blue.

Two lovers passed nearby, hand-in-hand,
arms swinging, strolling somewhere in no rush
already there where they wanted to be,
side-by-side in look-alike outfits,
faded jeans, bright red blazers, and sunglasses,
their wavy hair bobbing on their collars.

Were they men? Women?
Or male and female? Gay or straight,
I couldn't tell by their clothing, hair, or gait.

The way they sauntered and chatted,
lucid and gay, showed something only they
could laugh away, chirping sweet something
or nothings, inside jokes or secrets

they would keep till the end of time
or infinity, whichever came first,
cross my heart, till death do we part,
their levity revealed nothing about their sex
and nothing could quell their exuberance.

Was this the brave new world where gays
and lesbians can exhibit affection without fear?
Or, were they apprehensive yet didn't care,
unaware of the people walking there?

Walking by Lilacs

Gay or straight, little difference did it make,
several things were certain:
they were lovers, the lilacs lovely,
and I grateful to be among them.

Unlikely Places
Who would have guessed
birds would make their nests
in our dark, dusty attic
beyond the eye, nose, and reach
of predators out on the lurch
with no idea where to search?
You, too, have made our nest
in unlikely places, east and west,
always cozy, clean, and warm,
touched tenderly by the charm
of color-coordinated rugs on the floor,
daisies painted on a cabinet door,
blue valences, laces, and vases,
your love lingers in unlikely places.

Light and Easy

We walked alone along a wooded road
under a canopy of poplar trees
when we startled a timid, gawking toad
to hop into a cloister of daisies.
We stopped. You stooped. I knelt by the flowers
to pick a few for you was my intent,
a lively gift from these verdant bowers,
but your pliant fingers coaxed me to relent.
You helped me stand and stayed holding my hand
without speaking, you glanced and said so much
of you and me and how we could understand
each other with a light and easy touch,
as if to say, "don't pick daisies for me,
leave them be for other lovers to see."

Tap the Sky

Though
you can't catch sunny strands
or moonbeams in your hands,
I like to think I know why
you would try to tap the sky.

Still, it won't try to tap back
with a hardy, handy whack
unless it's cold or hot air
whacking you without a care,
piercing your back or chest clean
through the liver and spleen.

But the wind isn't the sky
to look up to or to try
to say you're way beautiful
in clouds, colors, hues so full
of birds and bugs in sunlight,
moon, Mars, and stars in the night,

so much so the Milky Way
beams bright all night and day,
I like to think I know why
you would try to tap the sky.

Careless Wish
Some scholars say nature abhors vacuums,
shunning them as lepers in the Holy Lands,
allowing them to exist only in labs
where their existence is up for grabs.
Others say, nature's biased as a whole
against empty spaces, filling every hole
ever made by worms, packrats, and oil rigs,
shovels, picks, and archeological digs.
Sometimes, I wish to live in vacuums,
empty spaces far from the daily scams
of pyramid plans and get-rich-quick schemes,
identity thieves and welfare queens,
but then, there'd be no space for crazy dreams
of stretching the status quo beyond its means.

Shaking Painting

The still-life painting
came alive at eight a.m.
Easter Monday morning
when the sunlight streaked
through my living room window
in stripes—
shaking shadows of vertical blinds,
swayed by the register's forced air
blowing from below the windowsill.

On the west wall,
the shadows rippled over
Denise Koch's watercolor painting
of a bluff overlooking Lake Superior.

The shadows shuffled the sunlight
to show still-life evergreens
swaying slightly atop the brusque bluff,
while at the beach,
a piper glided to land on the sand,
static waves rippled, lapping gently
onto the smooth rocks and sandy shoreline.

Authentic Antiques
"The family that prays together
stays together,"Bishop Sheen had
told us, and we did for a while;
we prayed rosary at bedtime, Mom,
Dad, Sis, and I. Dad took the lead;
we responded through the decades
kneeling in the dark before the
buffet gazing at our candle-lit shrine,
two tall candles, two votives,
enough light to see three statues.
We focused mainly on the Sacred
Heart of Jesus, a handsome man,
silken brown hair bobbing at the
shoulders, beard and moustache
neatly trimmed, pleasant blue eyes,
finger tips pressing His heart to the
breast, as though it might fall. To
the left, His earthly father, Joseph
held Jesus the babe, Jesus sporting
a prince's crown. To the right, His

virgin mother as Lady of Lourdes,
stood atop the world with open arms
and bare feet, the left foot squelching
the neck of a gasping snake that
straddled the world. Today, I saw
similar statues at a booth in an
antique shop among World War II
weapons, M1 rifles, German Lugers,
and hara-kiri swords, a handwritten
sign declaring on fading blue cardboard,
"Authentic Antiques, 20% off."

So Little Time

We spent so, so little time with them,
our parents kept us for one-third our stay,
they grew older, grayer, and then?

The days whisked away, and we the children
watched Dad and then Mom go their way,
we spent so, so little time with them.

Our children came to our lives when
we struggled to work and make ends pay,
we grew older, grayer, and then?

They learned to walk, talk, then again
to shout at the passing of Christmas day,
we spent so, so little time with them.

Now we speak to them of goals to tend,
paths to wend. Where tomorrow and today?
we grow older, grayer, and then?

They turn to jobs, school, or friend,
we grow grayer, much grayer they say,
we spend so, so little time with them,
we grow older, grayer, and then?

Old Cottonwoods

Two stumps stood rooted in the easement
between our sidewalk and curb where two
cottonwoods had flourished though slightly bent,
old patriarchs somewhat stooped at their pew
standing vigil showing something good could
last, constant and comforting always there
through hard winters and gray days holding fast
as long as we can remember, always there.

Our town fathers declared the trees a threat
leaning gravely over the shaded street,
their gnarled, crooked backs a sure bet
to collapse in tandem at the feet
or heads of some heedless passers-by.

What were the odds the old trees would fall
right at the time someone walked or rode by
in a pumpkin on the way to the ball?
Don't misunderstand. I've never been one
to gamble regardless of the odds,
the house wins. Nor do I think it fun
to tempt the fates and tease the flighty gods,
but the old cottonwoods deserved more
for standing vigil in the easement
than to be cut down having aged three score
without ceremony or bereavement.

PART IV

Mother's Pall Malls

I wanted the pure pleasure that comes
with breaking the rules in polite seclusion,
and getting away with it, a boy's myth
conceived while watching the recreation
of my parents on cool summer nights
when their faces glowed in cigarette lights.

They sat serenely in the sun-porch,
content to be in the dark together
in a lover's compact, they burned the torch,
two against the world, lover with lover
pledged in silence to support one another,
if busy bodies gossiped about Mother.

She smoked. But only with Father in the dark,
inhaling the slender Pall Mall slowly,
succoring the sensation, a total lark,
her nose and cheeks glowed momentarily
before she puckered her lips to exhale
and blow the smoke up a straight trail.

Between puffs they spoke of when they courted,
how they broke other rules of decorum,
such as the times they swam unescorted
and their folks thought they were husking corn.

Mother's Pall Malls

Lucky for them, they didn't have to say
why they worked so much for no pay.
That was their first date, a true rendezvous
without chaperones watching what they do.
How about the time they skipped rosary
to sneak away to the Van Buskirk farm
where they joined other young people to see
a crop-duster in a biplane swoop the barn?

They had a good thing and I wanted it,
so I stole a pack of Mother's Pall Malls
hidden in a sack of yarn she used to knit,
tucked in a hole in one of the closet walls.
I begged my little sister to join me
in a culvert linked to a WPA ditch,
where we sat in the dark and smoked liberally,
doing bad to have the good, which was which?

I didn't stop to think of the consequences
while we puffed Pall Malls in hasty sequences,
before long, the culvert's air turned thick,
fuggy with smoke, my eyes itched and head spun,
I burped, then retched the baloney sandwich
mother had fixed for lunch. Where was the fun

in my head spinning like a Ferris Wheel,
burping the bitter bile of my last meal?

One sure thing, my sister wondered the same,
although she didn't retch or look too ill,
she grabbed my arm and punched it with disdain,
screaming, "how could you pull this stupid deal?
Mother will know!" She wiggled out the culvert.

Bitter, bitter mouth, stinging arm, spinning head,
slumping in the culvert, I waited for peace,
the serene calm I had hoped lay ahead,
only Mother came, stooping on her knees.
"Come home, *hito*," she prayed without sting,
"You've had too much of a good thing."

The Price of Big Boy Toys
I was one of those anxious little boys
who tired of his father's homemade toys,
I told him so. I wanted a machine
like the big boys. Time it was he weaned me
of homemade toys like the spinning steel hoop,
pushed by a stout wire bent in a U-loop.

"Okay! Whatever you say!" He blurted,
with a broad, happy grin he asserted,
"You want big-boy toys, that's fine by me,
you can have almost anything you see.
Let's go downtown to Montgomery Wards,
Gambles, Muntz's Hardware, they got hordes
of burly, big boy toys for you to buy,
but, don't pay till you give them all a try.
Barter with the salesmen at all the stores,
nothing better to save money than price wars,
and don't offer anymore than you've got,
big boy toys cost a whole heck of a lot."

I was surprised and thought he'd be sore
I didn't care for homemade toys anymore,
yet, he wasn't gruff or mildly peeved,
actually, he appeared to be relieved
and went on to say, "cash is the best way
to bargain to bring down the price you pay.

Don't count on me to float you a loan,
you'll have to find a job and work to the bone,
that's the high price big boys have to pay,
they slave away for big-boy-toys for play."

The Price of Big Boy Toys

Found the toy easily, a three-speed racing bike,
the job was harder, a paper route hike,
two blocks south-to-north, and ten blocks up west,
where homes were snuggly tucked on a rising crest.
A compact route, one hundred customers
wanted the paper daily at their doors,
which meant, in theory, I could in four months
make 48-dollars for Mr. Muntz
to order the bike from Raleigh, England,
and within four to six months, it would wend
on ship, train, and truck to Muntz's Store,
in fact, the time needed was much more.

Daily, I folded each paper with care
in a square to pitch a short way in the air,
tossing the paper right at the front door,
while shouting like a pro golfer—fore!
Delivering papers was a piece of cake,
even fun and games for its own sake,
the real hard work was in climbing the hills
to collect from folks who didn't pay their bills.

There was Homer Meiser, the Nash car dealer,
who faked it as a rich wheeler-dealer,
when I approached him to collect at his house,
he stole around back, like a sneaky mouse
stealing cheese from a smaller mouse.

Yep! You got it! He was a stingy louse
who claimed, when I found him in the backyard,
"I'm not a niggardly, nefarious petard,
but, my ads in the paper should pay
for a free subscription! Whatta ya say?"

I couldn't support his caper,
I still had to pay for his paper,
so what could I say to the old geyser

The Price of Big Boy Toys

who made it big by being a miser?
I complained about him to my father,
who grinned broadly again, "so why bother
your head off? Sometimes you gotta bite
your tongue, keep your trap shut good and tight,
and hope your tongue doesn't bleed out your lips,
which you check with a brush of your fingertips.
Why talk to me? Go see your bossman,
tell him about Meiser, as calm as you can."

When I told Pinky, the circulation boss,
he shrieked in sharp, shrill spikes, "ah, hogwash!
Don't care! Moogie, Mongoose, Auggie, or Alph,
even the Good Lord Jesus Christ Hisself,
He's gotta pay! Or you gotta pay for him
if you give in to the old goat's whim.
Pinky sent me to Meiser's office downtown,
advising me not to scowl or frown,
because his secretary will surely pay
if I approached her in the big boy way,
saying nice things about her hair and dress,
giving her fresh-picked flowers for her tress.

In my mind, big boys shouldn't stoop to lie,
and that's precisely the reason why
Meiser's secretary, Dula Carruther,
didn't believe me. She called my mother
to get down to the truth to see,
if Boss Homer Meiser had paid me.
Mom gave Miss Carruther a piece of her mind
about men like Homer Meiser, "the kind
that gets rich on other people's money,
and are so tight, it isn't funny.
He won't pay for the paper to my boy,
who's working to buy a big-boy toy."
Miss Carruther hung up, burning hot and cross
for having to cover for her stingy boss,

The Price of Big Boy Toys

She made me feel like a common crook,
although I was playing by the book.
She doled out coins, counting dime-by-dime,
expecting me to hunker down each time
to know what it's like to succor on lime.

Then there was Mrs. Concha Cordova,
a World War Two widow, eligible by law
for a few veteran's benefits, not much
to help pay rent, utilities, and such.
She waitressed at the Silver Moon Café
and normally could pay me straight away,
"But now," she sighed, "the mines are closed down,
the big tippers, the miners don't come around,
but in a month, if you let my bills rest,
I'll have enough to pay you with interest."
Now I felt bad, a chintzy, craven cad,
rather than simply an ambitious lad,
striving to make cash to buy a big boy toy,
but, bilking widows? Holy cow! Hoy boy!
Dad's advice with the widow worked well,
I didn't fly off the handle pell-mell,
instead, I bit my tongue, bridled my greed,
and afterwards, my tongue didn't bleed.
Of course, I couldn't charge her interest,
that way I slept at night and took my rest.

What a weird, warped place, the big boy world,
where weird contradictions whirled:
the rich make it big off the little guy,
the poor pay more without a sigh.
What got my goat were the deadbeats,
the gay-blade sports, the crass cheats
who'd forgotten how small boys have big dreams
to be like big boys and play with machines.

The Price of Big Boy Toys

To their credit, they paid within nine months,
and I could finally pay Mr. Muntz.
He took the cash and ordered the bike same day,
mentioning "there would be a delay.
The Teamsters in New York are on strike
against imports like your English bike,
'Buy American,' they say, it's your duty
to support our workers to keep us free."

I waited for the bike more than one year,
during the duration it became clear
just how high the price of big boy toys was,
worse than drinking weak coffee without a buzz:
taking bull from subscription collection cheats,
hunkering down to appease rich deadbeats,
only to find when it's too late,
buying the bike sucked me into a debate:
buy American. Support the union cause,
Bilk the widow? These gave me pause.

I was ready to throw in the towel,
knowing that quitting would only trowel
and cowl the problem, but it would stay,
I'd be throwing hard-earned money away,
like living in a house and paying rent,
you've got nothing to show for what you've spent.
Needless to say, I was blue, down in the dumps,
when I received a call from Mr. Muntz:
"Come, get your bike. It's a beaut'!
Take her home. Run her through the chute,
But say, after all your whining and pain,
can you ever be a small boy again?"

Mr. Muntz's question was too late for me,
the big boy job had wiped out the mystery,
the peace that comes when ignorance is bliss,
a sigh is a sigh, and a kiss is still a kiss.
The more I learned in the school of hard knocks,

The Price of Big Boy Toys

the less I liked some folks up-and-down the blocks,
except for folks like Concha Cordova,
who could and should set the standards for the law.

I discounted what Mr. Muntz asked,
for when I saw the Raleigh, I gasped:
deep burgundy enamel paint, chrome
rims, bolts, and brakes. Skinny tires from Rome,
sparkling spokes, a 3-speed trigger gear,
bright red reflectors everywhere.
Rode the bike home. Showed it to my mother,
she told my Dad and bigger brother
to watch me take the bike up First Street Hill
and see me speed down without a spill.
That I did. Rode up the hill sitting down,
then sped down faster than a rodeo clown
runs from a raging, rampaging bull,
tall in the bike saddle, I felt so cool,
riding astride my lean-and-mean machine,
scooting up hill, floating down in a careen,
a cool summer breeze puffing up my shirt,
I'd never felt so focused, so alert
I forgot about the problems of big boys,
and the high prices they pay for their toys.

Booting a Bike Tire

When a tire tread wore smooth as a bit
and its smooth surface developed a slit
from bouncing over potholes and sharp rocks,
tufts of grass, an occasional box,
booting a bike tire wasn't daft
if you'd troubled to master the craft.

I deflated the tube and removed it,
measured the length of the tire slit,
cut *that* length from an older tire,
by now, you must think I'm an inept liar,
but, I swear from the bottom of my socks,
throw in the prize from a Cracker Jack box,
I jammed that patch into the tire slit
and massaged it till it fit like a mitt.

Slid the booted tire onto the rim,
replaced the tube, then pumped with vim
until the tube billowed in the tire, and I could
mount the wheel with wrench and plier.

Back in the saddle seat, basking in the thrill
of cruising 'cross cactus, rocks, and the landfill
strewn with glass and trash, the City Dump,
when—Th-wump! Th-wump!—A hefty hump
bulged the booted tire, th-wumping the frame,
front fork and front fender, all the same,

the boot ballooned much too fast, it wouldn't last
long enough to ride back home, slow or fast.
Dismounted and examined the bulging boot,
the swelling slit, aneurysing to shoot
wide open into a burgeoning splat,
bursting the inner-tube, leaving it flat.

Didn't happen! I deflated the tire
before the boot bulged any wider,
and then pushed the bike, walking it back home,
watching the deflated tire weave and comb
among the sharp rocks, cactus, and glass
sprinkled over the rocky trail and grass.

Had that tire lost its vulcanized will?
Should it be relegated to boothill?
Whoa! Hold up. Boothill in the cowboy day
was a place you went to stay away
from working hard through the livelong day,
but a dead bike tire should get more time
to serve a boy as a boot and save a dime.

New Year's Eve Bonfire

Born in places everyone had to leave,
nobody knew who started the custom
of burning Christmas trees on New Year's Eve
on the baseball diamond in Van Houten.

We just did it, stripped the tree decorations,
packed them away lovingly, dragged the dry tree
to the snow-covered field in preparation
for the annual impromptu celebration.

We joined other boys stacking trees
as high as we could go, the smaller boys
climbing the swelling heap, handing-up
each tree from boy-to-boy until
the highest boy couldn't stretch or peep
over the top of our funeral pyre.

New Year's Eve sometime after nine
folks converged, one family then many
circling the pile of spruce and pine,
worthless, some would say, not worth a penny,
yet still worthy of one more festive time.

Try this: take a pine needle and break it,
put the broken needle to your nose,
close your eyes and sniff to smell the forest
anytime you want, any time you suppose
a Christmas tree has only one fit.

New Year's Eve Bonfire

The fire was ignited without hype
when the time was ripe. All who were coming
had arrived, talking heaved higher and higher,
yesterday's newspapers, flashing matches,
flames creeping up the dry boughs, rising
with the singing of carols, tentative
and then in leaps with the pitch popping,
needles crackling, the carols swelling,
first in Serbian, or maybe Greek, it didn't matter
much, but to sing in the new, burn out the old
in Italian, Spanish, what's done is done,
dust to dust, the past is gone, time to move on.

I forgot to mention the Lebanese
who blended well and chimed in with others,
like the few Filipinos, the Japanese,
all strangers at this moment brothers,
echoing some old rite to light up the night,
enticing the sun to come earlier at dawn
while the bonfire spewed its light.

Joy coursed through the coal camp crowd
singing around the Christmas tree bonfire,
everybody was okay. Hope was allowed
and swelled among the multilingual choir—
refreshing and warm that was one good fire.

Though the fire burned bright, faces glowed red
from the lively flames in the middle of town,
nobody feared the fire would spread
across the coal camp and burn it down,
four inches of snow on the ground guaranteed
the fire would burn to the edge of its pile,
melting the snow on its fringe but then cede
turning on itself, dying after a while.

New Year's Eve Bonfire

Nobody knew who started it, the bright
burning of trees, the warm shared singing
to hold back the cold of winter's night
and to relish the promise of sparks
winging their way to Mars, maybe even
the stars, as if to join them. Did somebody
out there in the stars ponder this light of ours
bursting into view from our small place here?

Then, maybe no one noticed us at all
out among the stars. Or, over in Raton?
Maybe nobody heard our carols' call
nestled in the foothills. We were alone.

Really didn't matter who heard us,
anybody could come join the singing,
watch the burning, set aside old grudges
to celebrate our short time here, mingling
our varied languages and different ways,
burning out the old, singing in new days.

All Was Well
(For Bill Craig)

Last March I joined the legion of farmers
who gamble: plow and plant, rain will follow.
I did. It did. A spotty lawn sprouted in back
and front of my new home, right on track.

The gamble had paid off big on this slope
I called mine, where the soil had been scraped,
shoved away to build a new house of hope
for my family to take root and grow
as the lawn under the rain and snow.

Prepared the slope with a rented Bobcat,
a versatile machine, small and compact,
tractor, grader, and front end loader,
useful to spread the newly bought topsoil.

Yes, I bought dirt to cover the rocky slope,
and paid for manure from a corral,
to spread over the scarified pasture
after I'd mixed the dirt and manure.

Sowed the seeds the old fashioned way,
broadcasting them to spread evenly,
raking away occasional piles,
then I spread straw over the raw lawn.

Job done, I rested and watched from the porch
as a mist turned to snow and fell last March,
the lawn took a-hold, I could tell,
Lady Luck was with me. All was well.

All Was Well (For Bill Craig)

Yesterday, while snow fell in tiny chips
I cast more seeds over last year's spotty lawn,
and by noon, snow covered the swells and dips
of my yard, actually, the entire valley
was mantled with snow, and I could tell,
Lady Luck was with me. All was well.

This morning, my lovely white lawn
had changed, now a dark, feathery quilt
on the range, twenty-five blackbirds, at least,
at feast on the newly sowed seeds.

I burst out waving an old jacket!
They fluttered awry—a gigantic swoosh
clouding the sky,
only to return greater in number
while I sat almost in slumber
at breakfast, which they expected to do, too.

Again, I charged from the house,
yelling, "Shoo! Shoo!"
whirling the old jacket in repeat
of my flighty and futile feat.

Again they returned
after I let down my guard in retreat,
they wouldn't stay away.

I was not effective as a scarecrow
for all my flailing and foofaraw,
the blackbirds didn't take me seriously
and always returned more eagerly
bent on devouring the tiny seeds,
providentially strewn for their needs.

Weary and miffed, I built a real scarecrow,
hewing a crude cross out of two-by-fours,
dressing it with my old jacket and cap,
and planted it deep in the re-sown lawn.

All Was Well (For Bill Craig)

Ragged and rough, the scarecrow leaned
slightly to the south, its jacket lapels
flapped in the breeze as did the cap strings,
and to give it voice, I added cowbells.

The bold blackbirds adored my sculpture,
in fact, they adorned it everywhere they could,
perching on its stiff arms and capped head,
I'm not sure they understood
the scarecrow was to fill them with dread.

Aw, what's the use? They wouldn't stay away
though law and custom gave me some say,
the blackbirds behaved as though their needs
entitled them to the tiny seeds.

I control little of my lawn or lot
though I can claim to have bought them
in thirty years when the mortgage is paid,
I'll have three pages in legalese detailing
in degrees the exact spot of my very own lot.

How can a man own the land, except
the work he puts into it—making him
a part of it—that can't be sold or bought
apart from who pays the lien for the lot?

Last year Lady Luck favored me with a lawn,
this year she favored the bold blackbirds,
yet, all was well for a spell. I had the home,
the lawn, and plenty of blackbirds to give us song.

Matters of Fact

"Not a pretty sight," Grandfather Joe said,
"Over the road, up the slope where the brook
pops out the ground. Where she made her bed.
You'll see, won't like it. Guess you gotta look,
suit yourself. Don't happen very often,
didn't know she was ready to give birth,
or, I would'a checked her first thing this dawn,
didn't know till I saw her bloated girth."

"O-oh, I'm so sorry," I droned in a tone I'd honed
to protect me from other people's misery.

"Feel like hell, 'cuz I should'a knowed better,
the way she sprinted and carried on so,
wished I'd shut her in the barn. Not let her
loose to graze carefree on the west meadow."

"No use blaming yourself.
No good comes from it,"
I advised, the boy counseling the man,
"bad things happen, in spite of a good plan."

"Plan?" Grandfather droned, "any plan would fail
to fix dumb luck....Should'a heard her wail,
groaning, moaning so, I wished she was dead.
Like wishing up a tree. She turned plumb pale,
laid on her side, wailed, and twisted her head
something awful, wailing on and on
hurting all over, till she was gone."

Matters of Fact

"Don't fret," I quipped,
"things could get worse yet."

"Should'a put her out'a her misery,
still was wishin' up a tree, hoping for the best
the calf would live. That was silly,
foolish really. Should'a put her to rest."

"Aw, don't worry," I consoled tritely,
"what could you do?
These things happen, as a matter of fact,
just nature handing her calling card to you."

"Well, go on. Best you see for yourself.
See if you're so cold when you come back
with all your talk 'bout matters of fact."

I left the house, not half as willing as before,
crossed the road of slippery, sandy clay,
stepped over the fence and thought some more
of the cow, after what Grandfather had to say.
Was he truly heartsick for losing her?
Que sera, sera is what he'd usually say.

Climbed the marshy knoll, grass soggy and soft
along the brook that actually babbles,
if you listen hard enough,
as the cold, clear water, spring run-off,
trickles down a creek speckled with pebbles.

Reached the babbling brook's head
where water pops out of the ground,
spotted the dead cow, a Guernsey
on her side, four hours tops,
not yet stiffened, flies raising a row
busy buzzing about, flocking around
her eyes, nose, anywhere mucus secretes,
hooves sticking out her rump, blood on the ground,
the clamorous flies clambering over her teats.

Matters of Fact

Shooed the flies away. They'd soon be back,
the babbling brook would soon stop muttering,
grass would grow higher, all matters of fact,
with one less calf, one less cow for milking
Grandfather would have to keep better track.

Don't know what I expected to see,
wished I hadn't come, like Grandfather
wishing up a tree. But, in fact,
I'd have to come back with Grandfather
to remove the cow. Wish I hadn't come.

Grandfather Joe
God bless the old guy,
he was the life of the
party, always was for
three-quarters of a
century. He was the
life, even though Mary
his wife, she died back
in 1962. He was still
kicking, kicking hard
tapping maple trees and
chopping wood when
we celebrated his
seventy-fifth: we gave
him whiskey and drank
his danelion wine. He
died today at ninety-two.

Breaking the Seal

"You gave me a bum pup. I want another.
His tail pussed a cyst and had to be cut,
not worth a damn for show, so don't bother
to brag about the defective mutt."

"Whoa. Not so fast," I tried to cool her down.
"You had no choice but to amputate the tail,
but he'll make a grand retriever. He's no hound
to bark up the wrong tree. You'll see without fail
he's got the blood of Jo Jo Jumper,
and my April; you'll see a champion romper."

"Had!" She injected abruptly, "he had
their blood till I put him to sleep."

"Put to sleep?"

"Euthanized. Injected. Call it what you will,
he wouldn't be worth a tinker's damn
with half a tail. Don't be talking 'bout skill."

"You...you killed the pup." I pulled away
adrift in denial, the pup slain.

"Don't look at me that way," I heard her say.
"You got no right to judge. All the same
you can't claim he was maimed,
prick of the needle, is all. His supple

puppy muscles relaxed even more,
he rested on the floor...fell asleep,
not a whimper, not a peep."

Still yet, I couldn't talk. I drew a blank,
her voice rattled while she prattled,
waking me from a bad dream.
I sank,
muttering, "beauty's in a retriever's poise
when you down a quail and he pursues,
weaving through the grass with hardly a noise,
and there's plenty pleasure watching him, too,
return that quail without a bruise."

"Bull crap!" She cursed. "Money's in the show.
April never made you dough. Nor me Jo Jo,
that's why I crossed over to a show pup
to cash in more than a winner's cup.
Now that the pup's pussed tail broke the seal
are you going to keep your end of the deal?"

"I did. Gave you the best, a spunky guy,
verified by the vet to be *crème de la crème*,
you thought so too, the most alert and spry,
you took him home, an unpolished gem.

Now you make a claim on another one,
but if he turned out flawed and wouldn't show,
I might as well give you bullets and gun
to kill the pup and be complicit in the blow."

Peeved I wouldn't give her a second pup,
she left, stopping by Moen's Meat Market
where she bought seven pounds of ground beef
wrapped in a packet, "Premier," she told Moen,
"to feed the whole lot,"
which Moen took to be her family.

She drove home to stew and wait,
unwrapping the raw beef to aerate
in a sunny window to speed its decay,
all the more tasty when prepared her way.
She waited. Meat rotted week-and-a-half
till Sunday morning when she fitted her gaff.

"Jack, you give her too much to think
she could coldly calculate such spite,
the Devil pushed her to the brink
twisting what's wrong into right."

"No, Marie, 'twas she and nobody else,
why side with her? You heard yourself
how she turned on the poor, little pup,
the Lord should strike me if I made that up.

B'sides, the Devil doesn't stalk the land
looking to give folks a helping hand,
'twas she shattered a bottle in a bucket,
smashing the glass into tiny, sharp shards,
adding ground beef from Moen's meat packet,
with gloved hands, folded the beef and shards
into meatballs used to kill the other pups."

"Jack, the Lord should strike me,
if I side with her. I meant to say
it's her way to care more for the looks
of a pup than the pup itself.

What I'm saying, she's cold hearted
as they come. They don't come any harder,
and she has the grit to think we're outsmarted
by her spiteful way to repay the barter."

"There's no way to understand what she did,
they were just pups bound to be grand retrievers.
Maybe dreams of fancy furs and big cars
bucked her resolve to wait for us
to leave to church as regular as stars,
then driving over, greeted by the chorus

of frisky pups who knew her to be the master
of their brother, dead now but nonetheless
they didn't know, greeting her affably,
tails wagging, forepaws pressing on the fence
while she fondled behind their floppy ears,

allaying any fears, massaging their scruffs
to lower their defenses, she handed them
her glass-packed meatballs, which they devoured,
grinding their guts....They were just pups."

From the Lamp Post

A solitary lamp post rises atop
a concave corner curb and casts bright light
on a vacant lot, good only for *Lap Top*,
or some other dog to irrigate and cite the
lamp post and vacant lot as his claim,
although nobody will dispute the site,
neither lot nor post appears destined to fame.

Two shoddy signs hang midway on the post,
double-pointed messengers of consequence,
27th Street with the most to boast
bisects the town in orderly sequence.
Old Farm Road disjointed by strip malls
is broken by blocks of new developments,
cul-de-sacs, and rip-rap retaining walls.

On sunny days I walk my dog *Lap Top*
by the lamp qua signpost and marvel
at the speed new houses crop atop
the once fertile prairie, the lamp post
serving as beacon, pointing in directions
of progress toward fallow fields scalped
and leveled, stripped of grasses where
snakes and rabbits had burrowed.

Of course, they'll have to move
or risk the crushing weight of the asphalt
linking buildings and houses, goading
the critters into neighborhoods by default
where they'll have to burrow in backyards,
culverts, or the cracks in uprooted sidewalks,
bearing indignities by pets standing guard.

A Jump-Start

He rose from the gray one winter day
as I drove slowly through the blustering snow,
a man in a suit waved me to stop,
I rolled down the window, turned up the heater.
"Car's dead," he said, "not for gas. It's a sop
on batteries, shorting out somewheres.
How about a jump-start?" He told more than
asked as though his cares preempted my affairs.

It was cold outside, snow swirling high,
the man did not look well, smile awry,
his tie dangled loosely almost undone.
'Might as well. Can't dance, too cold to plow,'
I thought clamping cables to post,
returning to my car, revving the engine.
He followed suit, then hollered a toast:
"Here's to a good man, a true Samaritan!"

"Why thank you," I replied turning bold,
thinking to make the compliment true,
"how 'bout a cup of coffee?...On me....
At the Hy Vee. Get us both out'a the cold."

"No-can-do! Gotta go see my doctor,"
he blurted, "something about a lump
on my liver. Doc told me to proctor
how I spend my time, but thanks for the jump."

A Jump-Start

"But, shouldn't you take the time
to ponder the view, sometimes I do,
to smell the roses so to speak
before you grow too weak?"

"Thanks for the help, mister, but no-thank-you,
I can't kick back anytime, like you do,
b'sides, I never could loaf and rest," he said,
"I'll have time when I'm buried with the dead."

His car window edged shut as he pulled away,
front tires slipping on the snow-packed surface,
and though I was slighted, he was right to say

he must not waste time. Leave here to get there,
do this to do that, go about his business
as I, too, must attend picayune projects
to fix, clean, and maintain things I possess,

bag old clothes for the Salvation Army,
cash in a coupon—buy two-get-one free,
mail-in proof-of-purchase for a rebate,
pick up bargain paint before it's too late,
open or shut the fireplace flue,
there's always some bit of business to do.

Hanging On
In April spring cannonballs into town
blustering, billowing, rolling through fast,
waking me as it passes outward bound
though I'm in no rush to leave the past.
Winter was just fine, long nights for reading,
short days for work, weekends serenely calm,
now, long days are stuffed with hoeing and seeding,
all manners and sorts of work, life moves on
in recurring patterns, rushing much too much,
jerking me out of last winter's calm clutch.

The leaves have it right, graceful in the spring,
quietly unfolding before summer,
changing light into energy to wring
and squeeze-out all the food light will confer,
kin to the magic that adds yearly rings
to their trees, not to mention the gifts of breeze,
of shade and shelter for idle flings
for pups, poets, and squirrels taking ease.

Without weekend breaks, the leaves work into fall,
leaping from their trees and dancing down streets,
cluttering brick walls and open halls to stall
their fall to decay before giving last treats.
Clumped in piles, they make great fun,
I used to jump and shower under them,
shuffle and kick'em, dragging feet on the run,
even then, when in the throes of decay
some managed to overstay their welcome
before they drifted away.

Hanging On

Nowadays like then, you can still see
laggards hanging on, pale tan, brown filigree
clinging to limbs, ignoring the call to fall;
others huddle in piles of shriveled husks,
flopping in the breeze with hope breeding gall,
waiting to be scattered by sudden gusts,
skidding across frozen plains of snow,
like grasshoppers out of time and place,
brittle shells of their former foliage.
The gusts flip some on their tips to cartwheel,
too frail to resist, too brittle to feel the thrill
of cart wheeling in the wind, they roll over
the snow not caring where they blow.
Others call it quits, wedging on a stone,
in a culvert, or where berms form a bend,
till all finally stop, cloistered or alone.

I'd like to be like leaves, busy and useful,
unobtrusive, I'd linger and loiter a while
after working all summer to shuffle
along curbs and allow children to pile me
in heaps with other leaves from trees
gone bare. I wouldn't care what happened to me,
burn or rot. Maybe I'd blow across the sea?
Maybe I'd hang on till next spring? We shall see.

www.ingramcontent.com/pod-product-compliance
Lightning Source LLC
Chambersburg PA
CBHW060415050426
42449CB00009B/1975